LITTLE STARS

STUDENT BOOK 1

Leonor Corradi and Cecilia Pena Koessler
Series consultant: Sarah Hillyard

Pearson

HELLO!

1 LOOK AND LISTEN.

3

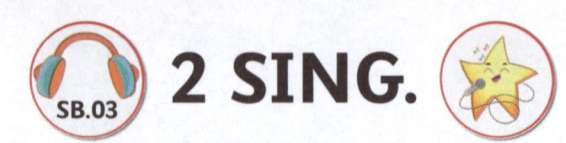

2 SING.

4

Hello Song

3 CHANT.

The Classroom Chant

5

UNIT 1 HELLO, CLASSROOM

1 LOOK AND LISTEN.

STORY TIME

6

7

2 SING.

Characters Song

3 LISTEN AND POINT.

Point to …
table, Oliver Octopus, Sandy Sock, Danny Dough

4 FIND.

Show me …
backpack

5 ROLE-PLAY.

I'm ...

11

6 CHANT.

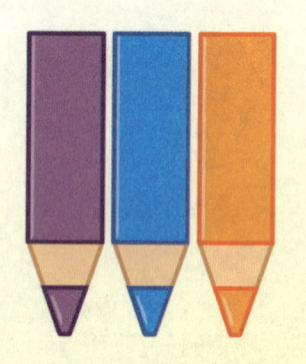

1, 2, 3

School Objects Chant

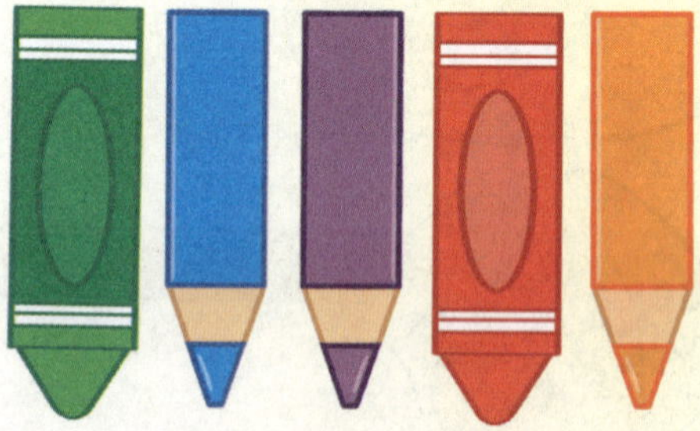

7 FIND.

Find ...
three, crayons, pencils

13

8 LOOK AND LISTEN.

14

LIFE SKILLS — helping others in need, making friends

9 STEAM.

STEAM CHALLENGE Can you use crayons on sandpaper?

Use a crayon to draw on paper. Press down harder to draw on sandpaper! *crayon, paper, sandpaper, press*

UNIT 2 I ♥ MY FACE

1 LOOK AND LISTEN.

STORY TIME

16

17

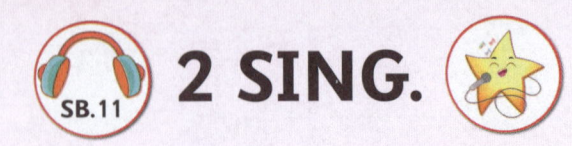

2 SING.

Face Song

3 SHOW.

Show me something with two eyes.
eyes, mouth, nose

4 WHO'S THIS? SAY.

20 Look at the eyes. Is this …?
mouth, nose, eyes

5 STICK.

Who's this? Is it …? Find the stickers. Now find Ms. Grass's eyes.
eyes, mouth, nose, I'm …

21

6 CHANT.

My Face Chant

7 COUNT AND SAY.

Look at this animal. How many eyes?
eyes, nose, mouth

8 LOOK AND LISTEN.

LIFE SKILLS — working together

24

9 STEAM.

STEAM CHALLENGE Can you draw your face?

Look at your face in the mirror. Draw it. Take a picture!

face, one nose, two eyes, two ears, one mouth, hair, happy face, angry face, sad face, silly face, mirror

UNIT 3 MY FACE, YOUR FACE

1 LOOK AND LISTEN.

STORY TIME

26

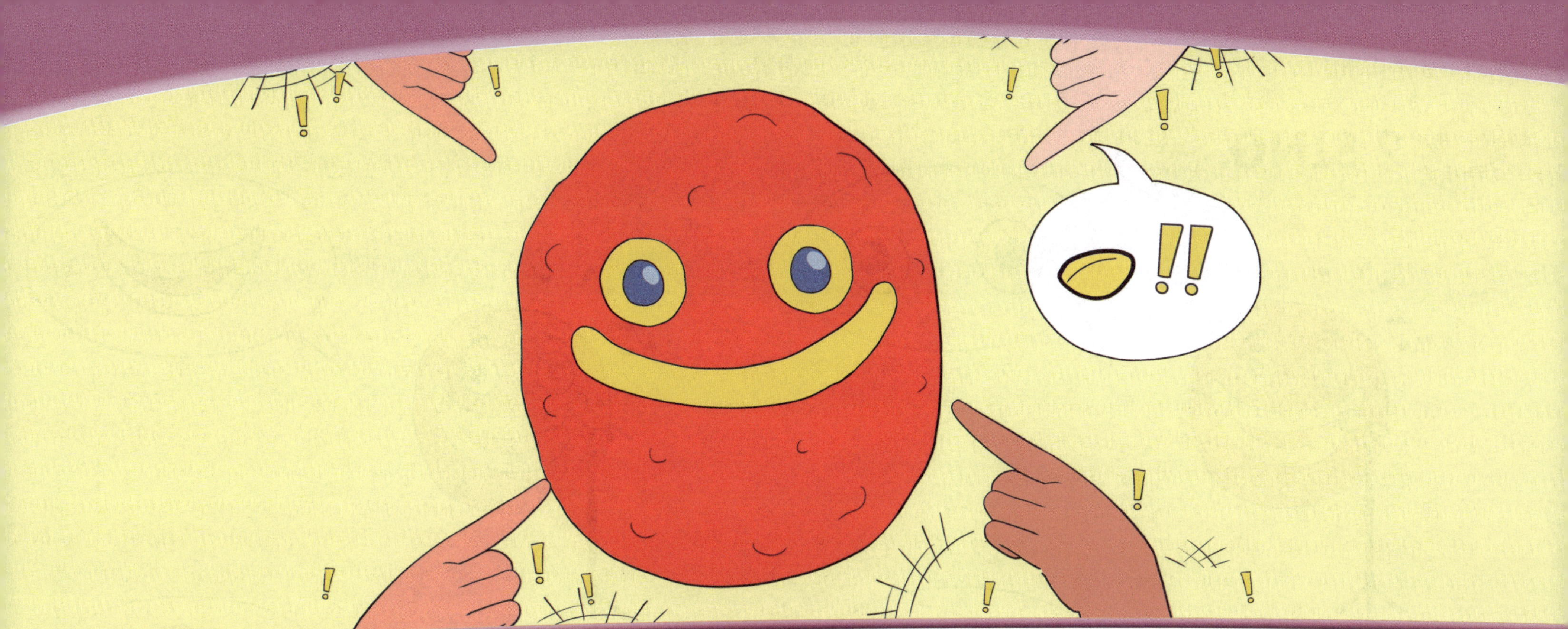

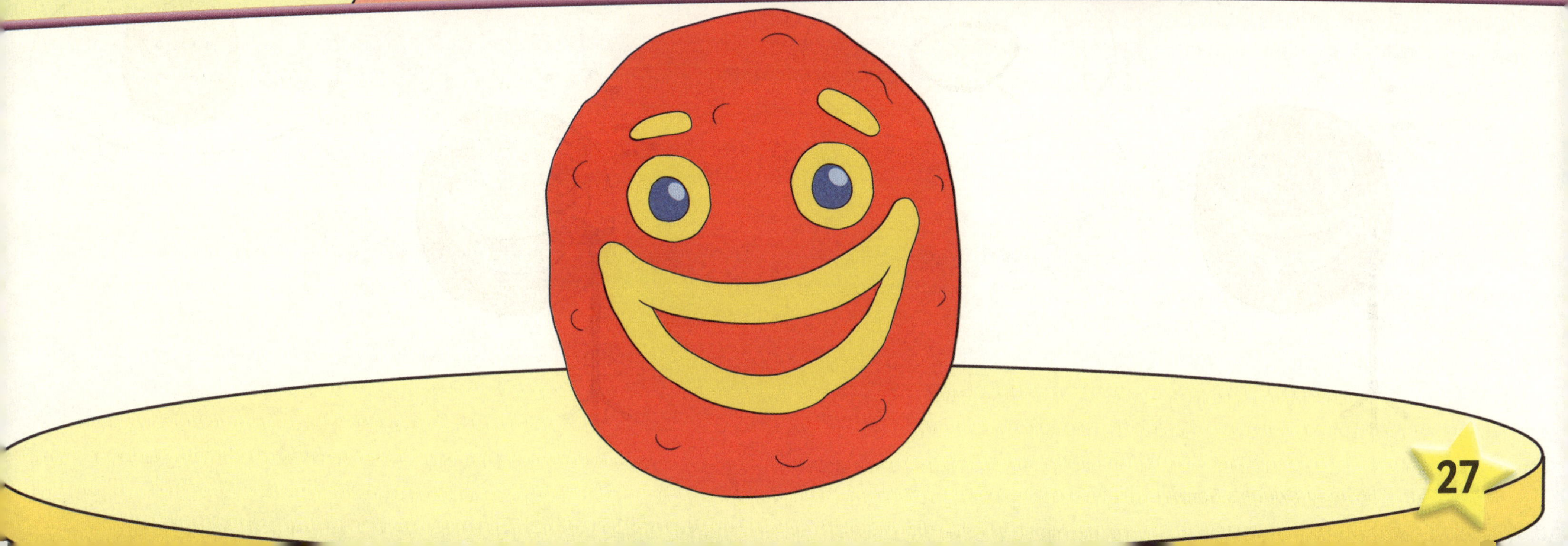

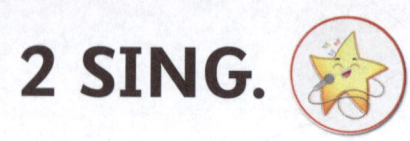

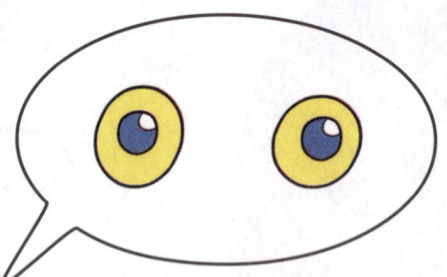

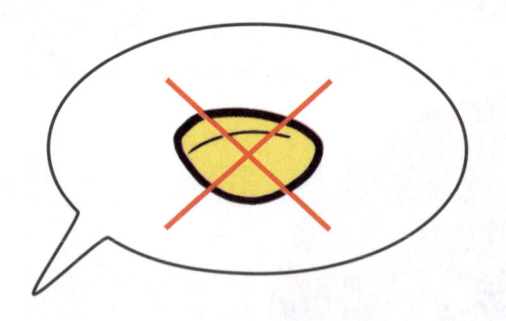

2 SING.

Danny Dough's Song

3 LISTEN AND POINT.

I have …
1, 2, 3, eyes, mouth, nose

4 CHANT.

30

I have Chant

5 LISTEN, DRAW, AND COLOR.

I have …
pencil, backpack, crayon, 1, 2, 3, red, blue, yellow

6 CHANT.

1, 2, 3

1, 2, 3

1, 2, 3

The Pencil Box Chant

7 COUNT AND SAY.

How many tables?
table, chair, crayon, backpack, pencil, 1, 2, 3

33

8 LOOK AND LISTEN.

LIFE SKILLS — understanding others' feelings, inviting someone to join in and have a go

34

9 STEAM.

STEAM CHALLENGE Can you draw with rainbow crayons?

Count 3 crayons. Tape them together to make a rainbow crayon. Draw!
1, 2, 3, crayon, rainbow, red, blue, green, yellow

35

UNIT 4 MY COLOR FRIENDS

1 LOOK AND LISTEN.

STORY TIME

37

2 SING.

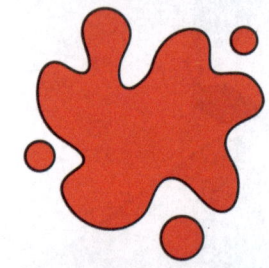

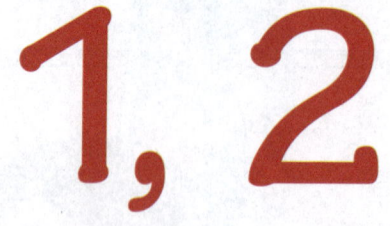

1, 2
2, 3

Color Song

3 LISTEN AND POINT.

Point to …
yellow, red, green, purple, blue, pink, sky blue

4 STICK.

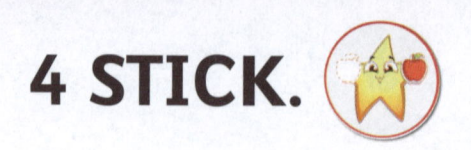

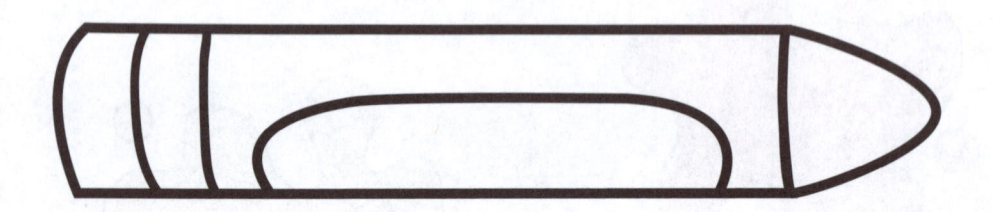

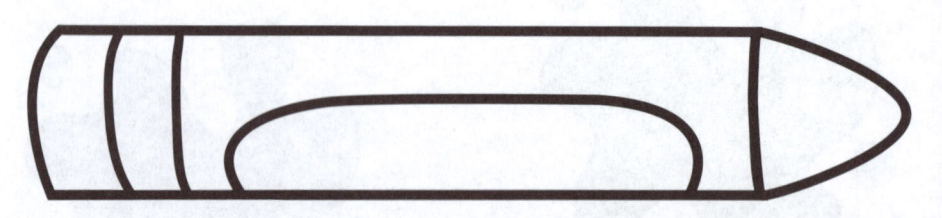

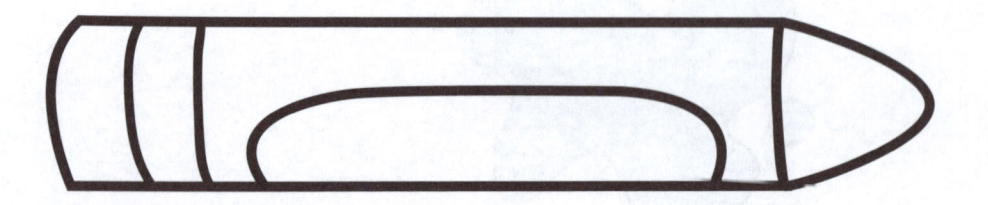

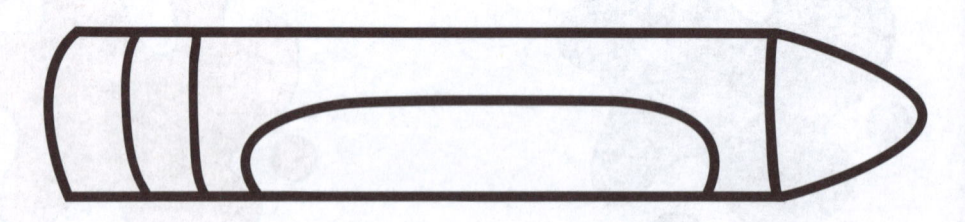

Stick …
green, purple, pink, sky blue

5 LISTEN AND COLOR.

The chair is sky blue …

crayon, chair, backpack, pencil, pencil box, table, blue, sky blue, red, pink, yellow, green

41

6 CHANT.

1, 2, 3

4, 5

Number Chant

7 LISTEN AND DRAW.

Draw …

8 LOOK AND LISTEN.

LIFE SKILLS — being quiet when appropriate

9 STEAM.

STEAM CHALLENGE Can you follow the pattern?

green, blue, green, blue. Follow the pattern. Finger paint!
blue, green, red, yellow, pink, sky blue, purple, paint, finger

45

UNIT 5 LET'S PLAY!

1 LOOK AND LISTEN.

STORY TIME

46

47

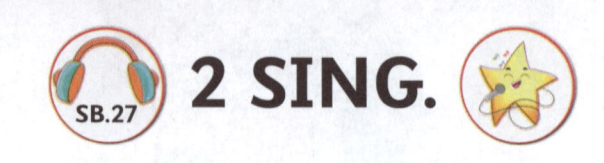

2 SING.

Ready, Set, Go! Song

3 LISTEN AND POINT.

Jump over the pink pencil box …
pink, blue, green, sky blue, red, pencil box

4 CHANT.

1, 2, 3, 4

Actions Chant

5 LISTEN AND TOUCH.

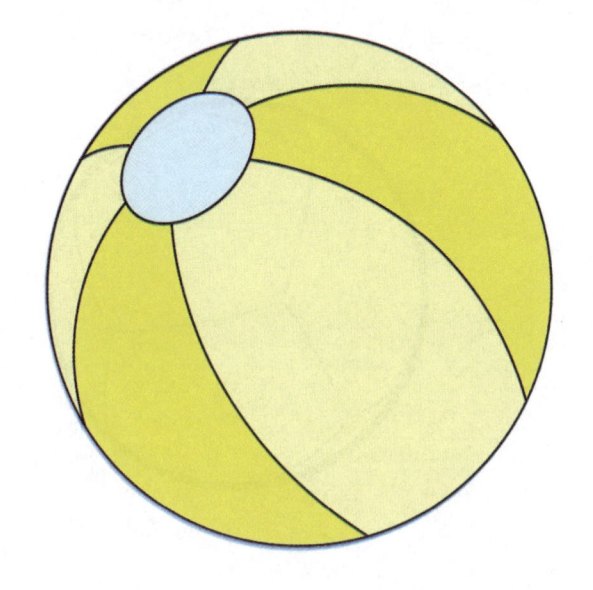

Touch …
car, train, ball, teddy bear

51

6 LISTEN AND COLOR.

SB.29

52

The teddy bear is red.
teddy bear, train, ball, car, yellow, red, sky blue, pink

7 LISTEN AND DRAW.

I'm … I have …
nose, mouth, eye

8 LOOK AND LISTEN.

9 STEAM.

STEAM CHALLENGE Which toy rolls down the ramp?

Which rolls down the ramp: the teddy bear or the ball? Color it. Trace the line down the ramp.

teddy bear, ball, car, train, ramp, roll

55

UNIT 6 SNACK AND PLAY TIME

1 LOOK AND LISTEN.

STORY TIME

56

57

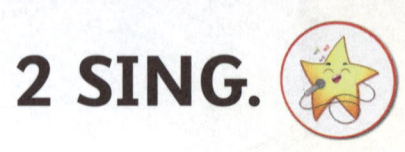

2 SING.

58

The Snack Song

3 LISTEN AND POINT.

Point to ...
water, tea, orange juice, cereal, cookie, fruit

4 CHANT.

The Toys Chant

5 LISTEN AND COVER.

Cover the doll ...
doll, ball, teddy bear, puzzle, car, block, plane

61

6 STICK.

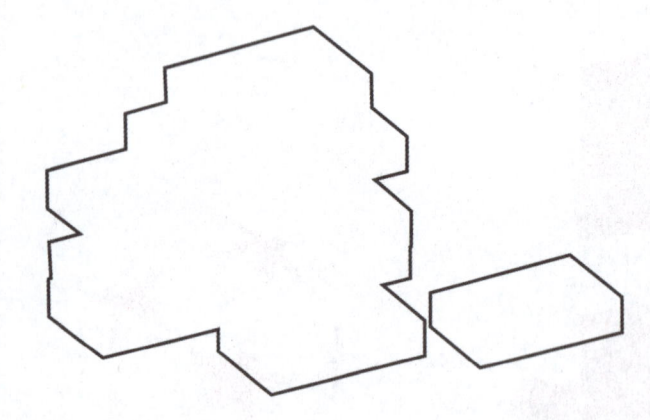

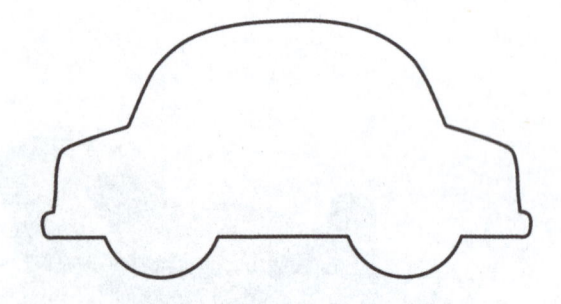

62

Stick …
doll, teddy bear, puzzle, car, block, plane

7 COUNT AND SAY.

How many ...?
1, 2, 3, 4, 5, ball, plane, doll, block, puzzle

8 LOOK AND LISTEN.

LIFE SKILLS — being clean and neat and asking for help

64

9 STEAM.

STEAM CHALLENGE Is it sweet?

Taste the food. How do we taste food? Are they sweet or not sweet? Circle the sweet things.
cookie, cereal, lemon, tongue

65

UNIT 7 HAPPY BIRTHDAY!

1 LOOK AND LISTEN.

STORY TIME

66

67

2 SING.

68

The *Present* Song

3 LISTEN AND POINT.

Point to ...
lion, cat, dog, rabbit, elephant, tortoise, octopus

4 COUNT AND SAY.

70

How many …?
dog, lion, frog, rabbit, elephant, cat, tortoise

5 LISTEN AND COLOR.

The frog is …

frog, lion, dog, cat, elephant, tortoise, rabbit, pink, blue, green, sky blue, yellow, red

71

6 CHANT.

72

The Size Chant

7 LISTEN AND DRAW.

Draw …
big, small, ball, dog, pencil

73

8 LOOK AND LISTEN.

LIFE SKILLS being polite and being kind to others

9 STEAM.

STEAM CHALLENGE Can we build big and small houses for our toy animals?

Frog can't find its house. Is the frog big or small? Draw the frog in its house.

big, small, house, cat, lion, rabbit, dog, elephant, tortoise, frog

UNIT 8 FAMILY DAY!

1 LOOK AND LISTEN.

STORY TIME

77

2 CHANT.

The Family Chant

78

3 HANDS ON.

Hands on …
baby, mom, dad, brother, sister, grandpa, grandma

79

4 LISTEN AND CIRCLE.

I have …
mom, dad, brother, sister, grandpa, grandma

5 SING.

I Like Song

6 LISTEN AND DRAW.

I like ... I don't like ...
blue, sky blue, purple, red, pink, yellow, green

7 STICK.

☺ ☹

*I like ... I don't like ...
lion, rabbit, elephant, tortoise, frog*

8 LOOK AND LISTEN.

LIFE SKILLS feeling proud and feeling happy for others' achievements

84

9 STEAM.

STEAM CHALLENGE Can we make a family for Danny Dough?

Make dough. Make a family for Danny Dough. Draw the member of the family you created.

dough, mom, dad, brother, sister, baby, grandpa, grandma

85

LITTLE BOOKS 1

- SB.9 — WHO ARE YOU?
- SB.13 — MS. RED GRASS RIDING HOOD
- SB.20 — A RAINY DAY
- SB.25 — PAINTING DAY
- SB.32 — NOT A COOKIE!
- SB.36 — LET'S HELP MS. GRASS!
- SB.43 — THE NUMBER RHYME
- SB.49 — SANDY SOCK AND THE THREE FINGER PUPPETS

WHO ARE YOU?

87

88

MS. RED GRASS RIDING HOOD

89

90

A RAINY DAY

91

92

PAINTING DAY

SB.25

93

94

NOT A COOKIE!

95

96

🎧 LET'S HELP MS. GRASS!

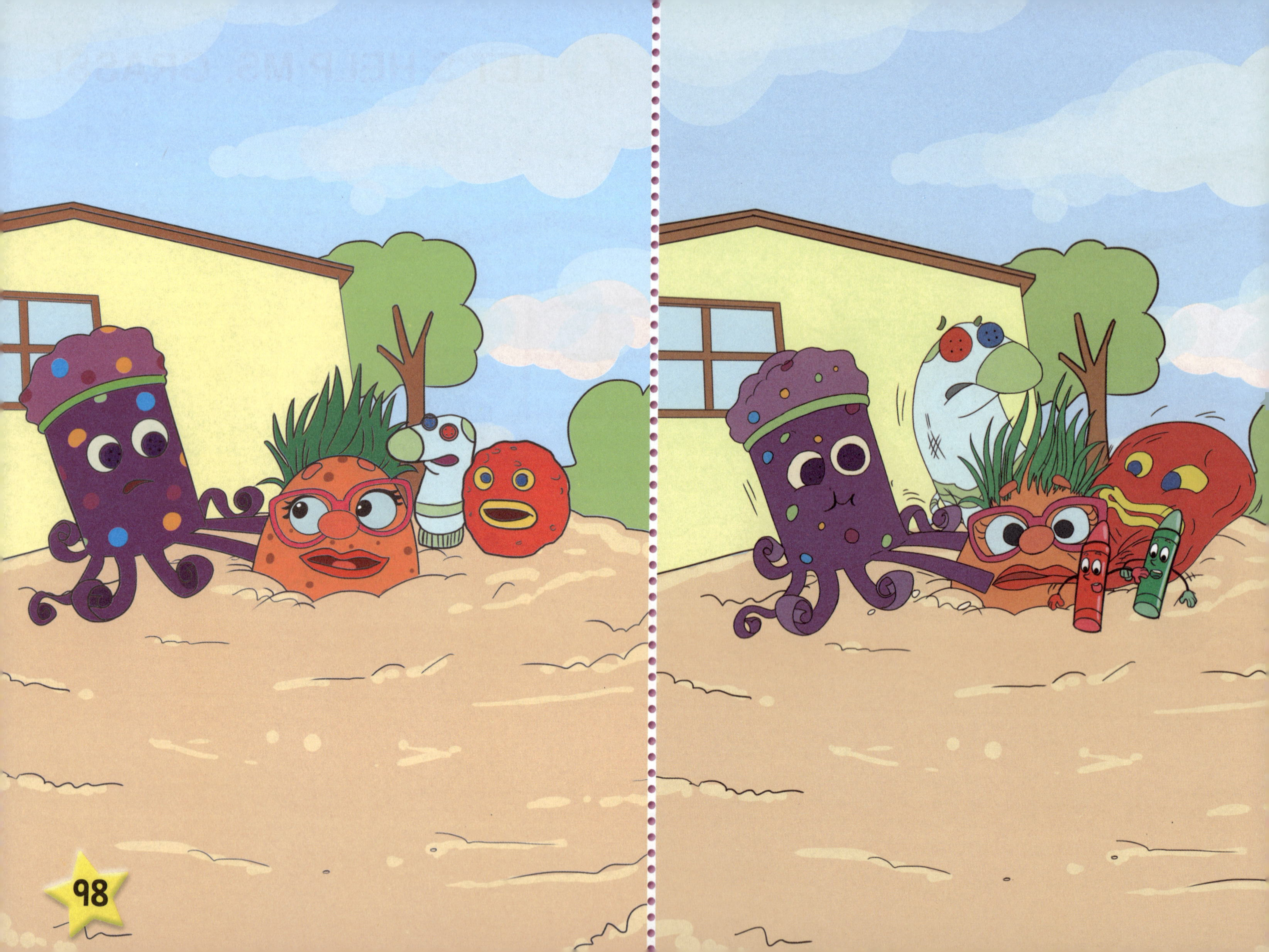

THE NUMBER RHYME

100

SANDY SOCK AND THE THREE FINGER PUPPETS

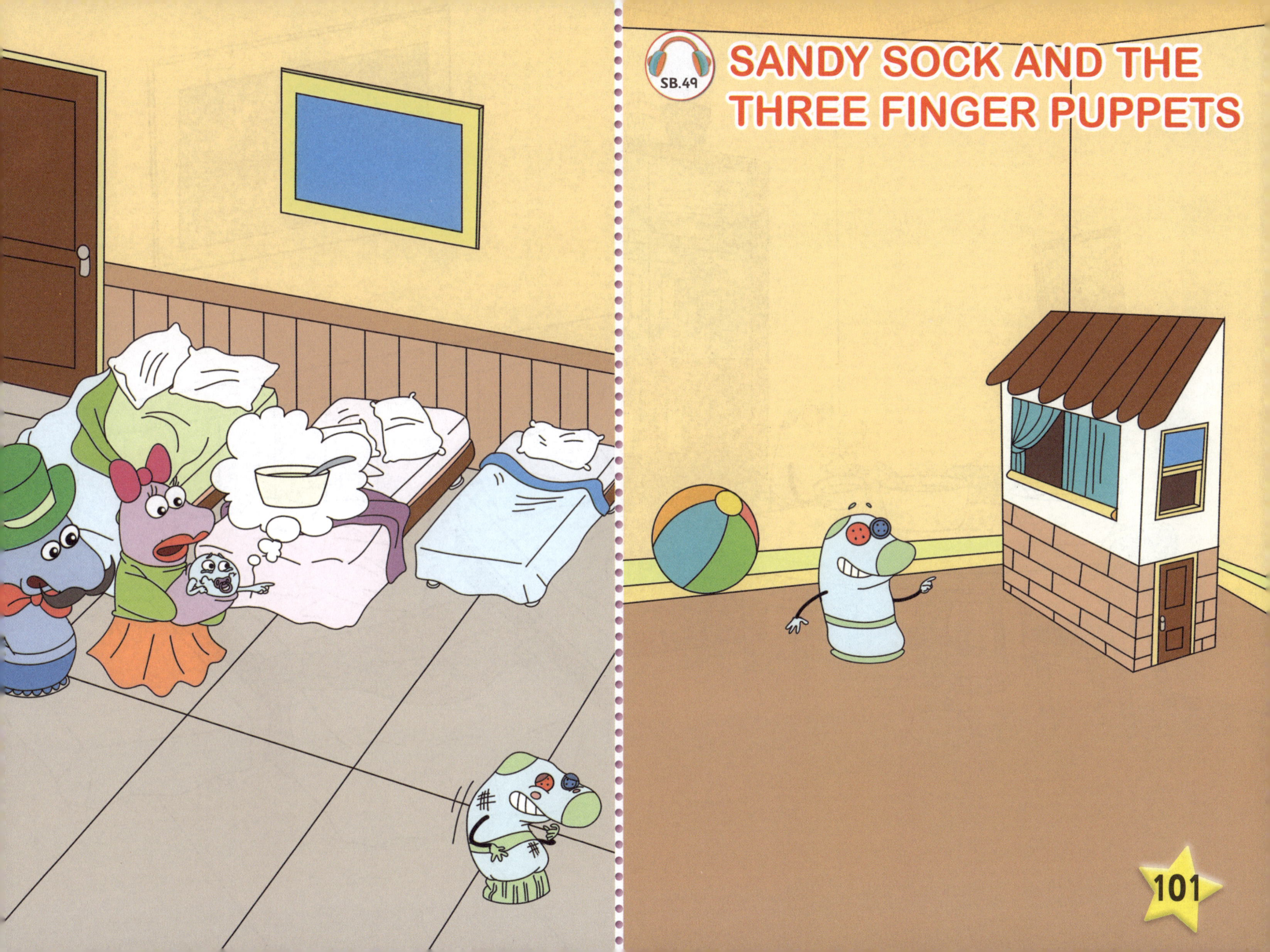

101

102

LITTLE STARS 1

HAS COMPLETED LEVEL 1!

TEACHER

GOOD JOB!

Pearson

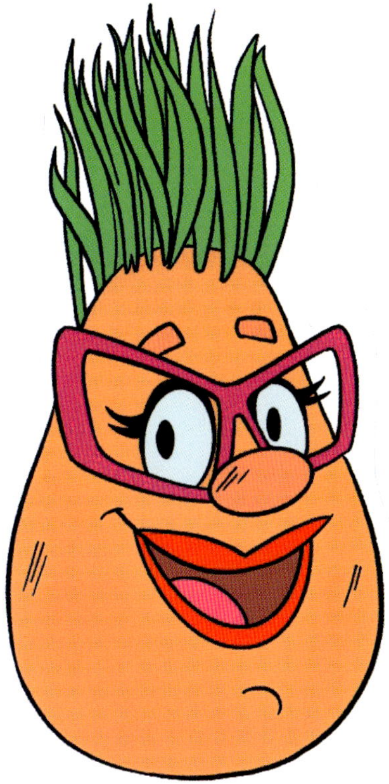

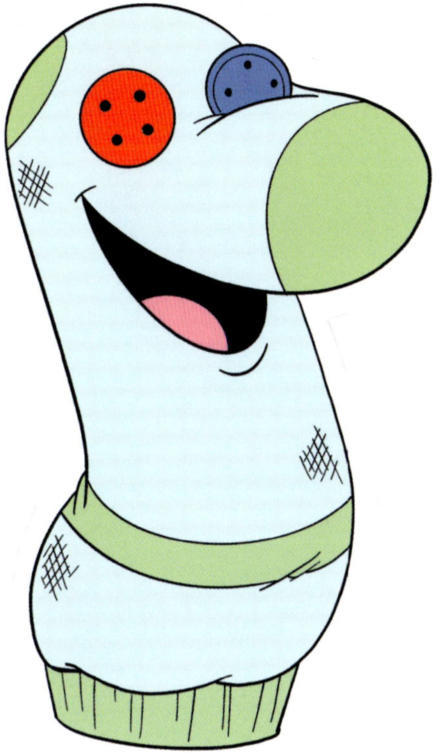

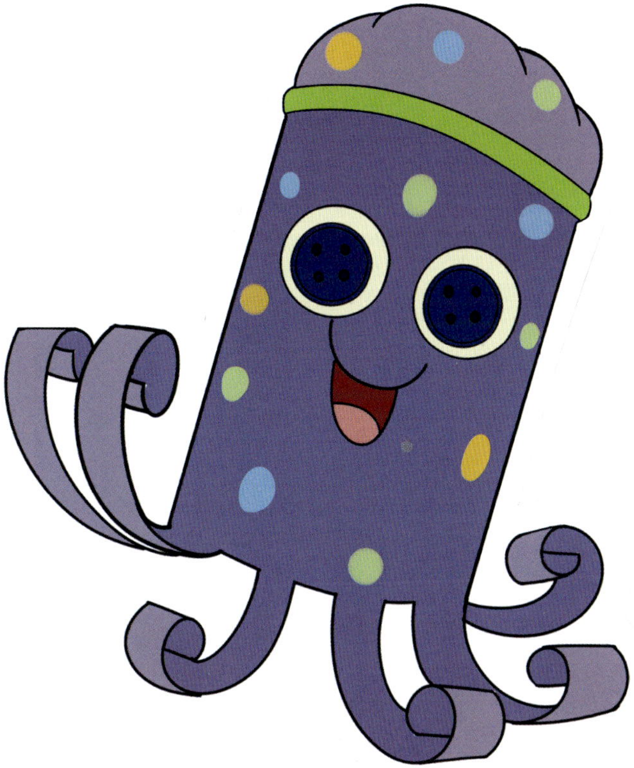

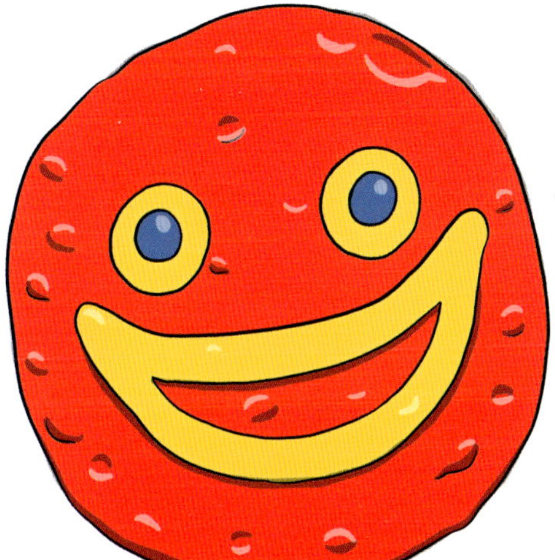

STICKERS

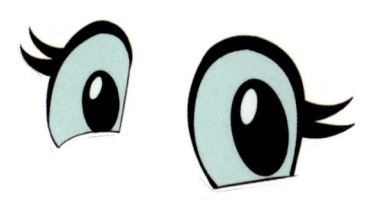

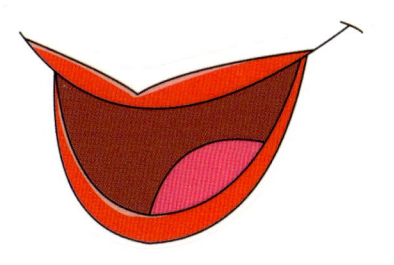

UNIT 2

UNIT 4

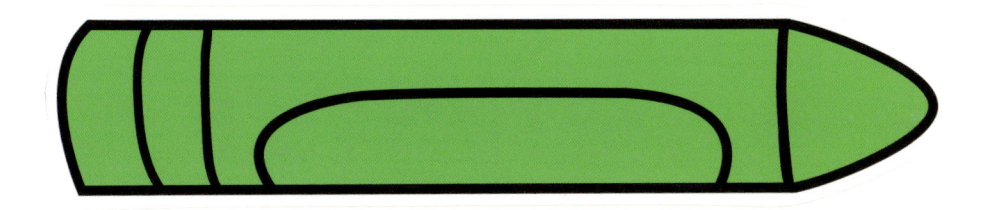

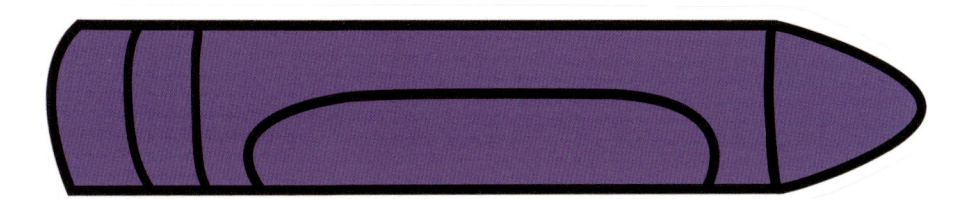

UNIT 6

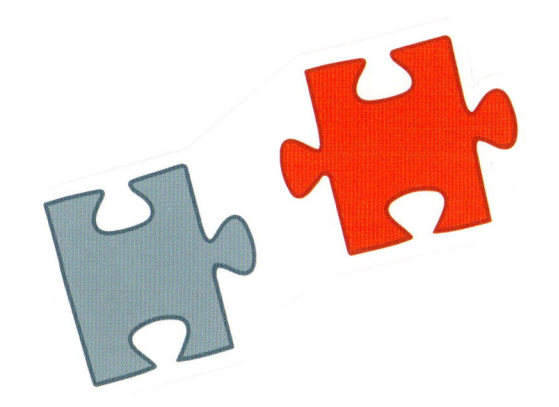

UNIT 8